You may call me Lance

You may call me Lance

Story of Lancelot, a Rescued Cat

Leo Burstyn

You may call me Lance

First Edition, 2021

ISBN: 978-1-9991048-0-1

DEDICATION

To the veterinary professionals who keep all our animal friends healthy and happy. We should remember that medicine treats humans, but veterinarians cure humanity.

CONTENTS

Introduction........1

Foreword........3

Chapter 1: My name is Lancelot and I am a cat........5

Chapter 2: My first adopted family (Melita and Ruben)........8

Chapter 3: My home is my playground........11

Chapter 4 Life is full of surprises (not all of them pleasant)........14

Chapter 5: My street life........16

Chapter 6: Interactions with hooman neighbours........20

Chapter 7: Beginning of professional life........24

Chapter 8: My mission........28

Chapter 9: Quality control........33

Chapter 10: I am not a "Puss in Boots"........36

Chapter 11: I am in the movies........38

Chapter 12: My little friends........46

Chapter 13: I am a happy cat........50

Epilogue........52

Acknowledgments........53

INTRODUCTION

Lancelot, that Most Noble Knight

Many cats lead extraordinary lives, but not many are lucky enough to have their adventures documented through the eyes of someone who truly understands them. Sir Lancelot is a legend of a cat, a YouTube star in the Helpful Vancouver Vet videos, and a valuable member of a veterinary clinic's staff. And now you can marvel at the story of his life as told in his own words and written down by the father of the helpful vet himself, with exclusive access to one of Vancouver's most regal and bewhiskered internet celebrities.

Every person who has adopted a cat from a shelter wonders at some point—usually while looking into those enigmatic eyes half-closed in contentment—where did you come from? What was your life like before we met? What hardships did you overcome to, finally and deservedly, land in the luxury of my lap? The cat rarely replies. That is why this book is such a marvel. A chance to see the world through the cat's eyes. It is based on personal interviews with Sir Lancelot (with interpretation helpfully provided by members of staff at the veterinary clinic where he resides).

Follow the exploits of a young cat as he deals with growing up, adjusting to surviving on the streets and back alleys of a large city, and eventually finding his forever home all seen through the eyes of the phlegmatic titular feline. This is a story of loss, adventure, redemption, and observational humor that is great for children of all ages, as well as adults who have a special place in their heart for cats and all that cats do.

Uri Burstyn
Medical Director, Arbutus West Animal Clinic, Vancouver, BC, Canada
April 2021

FOREWORD, OR HOW IT ALL STARTED

When you first meet Sir Lancelot of Arbutus, it takes only a few seconds to fall under the spell of his terrific personality. His remarkable career from little fluffy kitten to "The Boss" is inspiration for all cats, and maybe some of us humans as well.

Lancelot has the endearing quality of being able to make everybody comfortable and relaxed around him. Within a minute of meeting this cat, I felt an immediate connection. Despite his huge size, he is not scary or intimidating. On the contrary, most people would like to know him better.

Lancelot does not love *all* animals, but he values them all, even dogs.

I was fortunate to have Dr. Uri as an interpreter who could translate from Cat-Speak into Human. The more I got to know Sir Lancelot, the more I felt compelled to tell his story. To my surprise, Lancelot does not have a shred of vanity or snobbishness, and only a few minutes into our conversation, he told me: "You can call me Lance."

Now, let us follow Lance on his remarkable journey.

CHAPTER 1

My name is Lancelot and I am a cat

Mom

I've always known that I was a cat, but during my early life I had lived among so many critters and hoomans, it was easy to get confused about my identity. I've been called skunk, panther, ferret and many other names, some of which are better forgotten, but I've always known deep down that I was a cat. It is not too difficult to remember who I am, because I know where I came from.

My furry mother was a cat.
She was fluffy and warm, but I could not see her or anything else in the first days of my life. My main concern in those days was food, and the smell of milk was always in the air. To get to my feeding station it was necessary to push some other fur balls aside. Little did I know that they were my brothers and sisters. When I got too pushy, some big, strong paw would put me in my place.

After a while, I started seeing grownup cat of the same black and white colouring as myself. Mom fed and licked and groomed us, and we were so happy to be close to her. It was she who gave us our first life lessons.

I was a happy kitten, in spite of always being hungry. Mom forced us to share food to make sure every one of us got enough. She was a very fair-minded cat. Mom took good care of all her fluffy children. She was also very good at keeping us in line. We all did our regular grooming and shared meals with Mom, or should I say, had Mom as a meal. Her milk was sweet.

When we grew bigger, we started exploring the big world around us. Soon enough, I noticed that my family was not the only residents of our house.

Our clan consisted not only of cats, but also huge creatures called hoomans. Several of them shared our dwelling. The hooman who gave us food was Granny. She was always around the house and she kept Mom's bowl full of food and cleaned our toilet. Granny shared a room with Grandpa and something called TV. Grandpa spent most of his time in their room. Sometimes, our Mom would go watch TV, sitting on Grandpa's lap and purring, but she would never cuddle up to Granny. It did not make a lot of sense, because Grandpa never gave us any food.

We also had two grownups in the family, the Lady and her husband. They would leave every morning for what they called "work," and had little contact with our cat family. The only creatures that our Mom was close to were two boys, one small and another much bigger. They would play with Mom, and even pull us from our den to play with us as much as we could wish for.

Maybe it does not sound to you like a big deal, but it is time to talk about Mom's reputation. She was extremely strict and had a quick temper. Most hoomans visiting our house were afraid of her. Mom was from a proud family of guard cats. Every time the doorbell rang, she would run to the door and jump onto the bench in front of it. From this vantage point she would closely watch every person entering the house. Many people were charmed by her beauty, but they had to think twice before trying to touch her. She was very quick to strike anybody foolish enough to stretch a hand towards her.

One incident I remember should tell it all: One day, the Lady of the house got sick, and a doctor was called. When the doctor entered our house, Mom followed him to the Lady's room and immediately jumped on the bed. As soon as the doctor tried to come close to his patient, Mom started making growling sounds. It was similar to the roar that our cousins who live in a jungle or savanna would make.

The doctor froze in his steps. It was a terrifying picture: a little cat with an arching back, whiskers bristling and fearsome look on her face that did not leave any doubt that this fluffy beauty was ready to defend her family by any means. The doctor was forced to treat the Lady from a safe distance and gave her a necessary prescription without a physical examination. I think it was a smart move by the doctor.

I never had my Mom's temper, but I adopted her values—it is important to protect your family.

CHAPTER 2

My first adopted family (Melita and Ruben)

When I reached the age of majority, which is for kittens around two to three months, my family started looking for a new home for me. Some strange hoomans became frequent visitors to our home. Mom would not let any of them touch us, so they eyed our brood from a distance. Eventually, Granny would pick up one of us, and my brother or sister would go to perform a guard cat's duty with the new family.

Finally, it was my turn to go. A lady by the name of Melita came to our house. She looked the same age as Granny, and as I learned later, she was a grandmother as well. After a brief conversation with Granny, they put me in a box with a wire door. For some reason, they called this box a cat carrier. I thought it was a fitting name, and I felt flattered.

This was also the time when I got my own name. My new hoomans had the honour of deciding what to call me. As I mentioned, my mother had a pretty serious reputation, one you did not want to mess with. Did I mention that we looked alike, Mom and I? At only two months, I was already the size of my mother!

I did not inherit her character and temperament, but they decided to call me Lucifer anyway. Apparently, it's the name of the biggest, scariest cat there is. All my future adventures show that this name did not suit me well, but at that time, I did not have the slightest idea what it meant. In any case, we cats do not respond well to names like this. "Lucifer" lacked any high-pitched sounds, and I hardly paid attention to it.

My first trip out of the house was truly exciting. I experienced many new noises and smells. It was also my first ride in a car, and I was glad to observe life on the street from a close distance. When I entered my new home, I met another hooman that was living there, named Ruben.

I was excited to explore my new place. I was pleased that food and water were already prepared for me, as it should be, of course. Also, Melita took me to the toilet room, where everything was prepared for my convenience and to my satisfaction. I thought they were doing a good job of being hoomans and bumped Melita's leg with my head to show her that I approved and would not eat her that day.

I liked everything about my new place. It was smaller than the previous one, but it was my own. There were a lot of things for me to explore and enough cushions to lounge on, so I could start working on developing my meditation skills, every respectable cat's objective.

Both Melita and Ruben were very kind to me. It was the first time in my life I could watch TV. I still do not understand why they call it watching, when all I did was sit on Ruben's lap and purr with my eyes squinted shut to demonstrate my approval of the proceedings and my state of complete relaxation.

My new owners stayed home most of the time and we enjoyed each other's company. We did not have many visitors. Once in a while, a lady would come to our place and help Melita and Ruben with their chores. Her name was Nurse. She was very nice to me and I immediately liked her. On each visit, Nurse brought me some treats. Not that I was hungry, but it feels good when somebody cares for you, so I obliged her by eating them all.

CHAPTER 3

My home is my playground

As a young cat, it was my job to run around the house and knock down any items not properly secured. It is every cat's proud duty to do quality assurance around their hoomans' homes this way.

While running around the house, I found many places where I could hide and wait for my prey. All the rats, mice and wolves must have heard that there was a guard cat coming to live in our home, because I did not see any.

To help me stay sharp and practice my hunting, Melita brought home some "toys." There were all different kinds, and I would play with one or another, always changing which ones I liked, to keep the hoomans on their toes, as well as any wolves who may have been watching me. I never tired of catching and releasing my "toys." It was good exercise and a great way to share my "prey" with Ruben. He sat most of the time and could not catch anything by himself.

The wide windowsills in our home became one of my favorite places. From these observation and lounging platforms, I could watch what was going on outside. The trees in front of our house inspired my imagination. I dreamed about all the fun it would be to climb the trees. For some reason, I had to share the window ledge with plants. It was difficult to maneuver among the pots, and inevitably, I got so focused on the little birds playing in the tree, that I pushed one of the plants with my hind leg. Melita heard the noise of the breaking pot, and we had our first quarrel.

When she noticed the broken pot and soil spilled all over the floor, Melita grabbed the first thing she could find, which was a newspaper. She also became quite vocal for some reason. Seeing my owner approaching me with a paper in her hand, I was not completely sure about her intentions, but decided not to take any chances. I sprinted to the next room without delay. Ruben was watching his TV there, and I jumped onto his lap.

By the time Melita came into the room, I was completely relaxed on my master's knees, and already starting my customary purring. I closed my eyes as my owners had a rather expressive conversation. It was the end of the conflict, and I still do not know what Melita had intended to do with that newspaper.

Overall, I enjoyed living with my new family. We had some conflicts, but our love for one another helped us to resolve them, and we never held grudges for long. From dawn to dusk, I hung out in the living room and kitchen. At night, I would watch over my family in their bedroom.

During the day, Melita kept the bedroom door closed, which irritated me greatly, and I could not hide my true feelings. I composed several epic poems on the topic, which I would recite under the door. It is a well-known fact that cats are great poets, and it is a shame more people do not appreciate feline poetry. Occasionally, I would try to open the bedroom door during the day, but for a long time I did not succeed.

It bothered me, what they were hiding from me. Everybody knows that closed doors contain great and wonderful secrets, so I was relentless. It is funny, because at night I could not see anything special in there, so it must have been something really magical that only appeared during the day.

Finally, one day I got lucky. Cats are generally very lucky, which is why we push our luck so often. A casual paw push on the door made it open ever so slightly, but it was enough for me because I have lightning reflexes and can squeeze myself into any crack or box I see. Trust me! I usually walk with a slow, regal stride, but I can also be extremely fast when I feel like it. That is one of my favourite things about being a cat.

Within a second, I was through the door! I leapt onto the bed and looked around. Along the wall I noticed a big mirror and inside it a very large cat was staring back at me. This cat looked somewhat familiar, but I could not smell him. The cat repeated my every move. When I came closer, it became obvious that the cat lived behind the glass. I made the interesting discovery that behind the glass is another world, where everything is the same as here.

My life with Melita and Ruben was very good. I was never hungry and had many places to rest and many toys to play with. We cats do not make plans for the future, so I just enjoyed my life and worked on my hunting and ambushing skills. Everything was also going well in the world behind the glass. The cat that lived there was getting bigger too.

CHAPTER 4

Life is full of surprises (not all of them pleasant)

I noticed that my master Ruben had started changing his habits. He did not watch as much TV as in the past and was spending more time in bed. Nurse began coming to our place more often. One day, Ruben was taken away, never to be seen again.

Now it was only the two of us, Melita and me. She spent more time at home now. Melita's son and grandchildren visited us more often. I enjoyed these visits, because kids had always spoiled me and I could play hide and seek with them. Nurse did not forget me either, and I kept getting my treats.

But it became more and more difficult for Melita to take care of me. She could not keep my toilet clean to our usual standard and Nurse had to do it instead. Nurse also had to help Melita with her chores.

On one visit from Melita's family, her son picked me up and took me to their house. The first thing I noticed in this new place was a big red cat. They called him Joe. He seemed like a nice cat. We did not fight over food and treats, but he got to them first. It was clear to me from the beginning that I was in his home. As usual, I started exploring this house. I felt Joe's presence everywhere. It was a strange feeling, not being able to find a place in this big house where I could be comfortable.

While I was exploring, I came to a closed door. I pushed and, to my surprise, it opened and then closed behind me. I was standing outside, breathing in the fresh air! So far in my life I had never been outside. The smells and sounds were overwhelming. My instincts kicked in, and I made myself invisible by standing completely still and shaking my tail in the air so that I looked like a bush.

After a brief hesitation, I decided that the outside is all very well and good, but my duty as guard cat meant I had to go back to Melita's place. I was highly confident in my sense of direction, since like all cats, I always know where to go. So, I started walking.

CHAPTER 5

My street life

While I was walking along the street, it became clear to me that I was an invisible cat. Neither cars nor trucks could see me. Moreover, people on the sidewalk tried to step on my tail. Once I took a break on the steps of a house, and people still walked by me, nobody stopping to feed me or give me a scratch under the chin. With this understanding, I was extra careful crossing the streets and avoided collisions with hoomans.

There were many trees on this street. Under one of them I spotted a creature with a long tail looking for something in the tall grass. When I approached, the squirrel (I learned this name later) jumped on the tree trunk and within a second was looking at me from the top branch. So, animals could see me, and that was reassuring.

At the next corner, I looked down the side street and noticed a furry family, a mom and two cubs going into a back alley. I decided to follow them. From a distance they looked like cats, but when I came closer it was clear that I was mistaken. These animals were the same colours as I, but with a distinct white stripe on their back. They also had a distinct smell to them that I could sense from across the street. Luckily, Mrs. Skunk saw that I was also black and white, so we became friends and felt safe around each other.

By that time, I was a little tired and climbed on the roof of a small building to have a rest, because as a guard cat, I know it is my job to always find observation platforms to rest on. I liked the back alley. It was much quieter than the street. From my observation point, I saw Mrs. Skunk with her family walking along the alley, checking garbage cans for food (garbage cans are where hoomans put food to share it with other critters, which shows that hoomans are, generally speaking, a lovely bunch, even if a bit awkward at times).

My inspection of this back alley was interrupted by a brief rainstorm. It was my first direct contact with water coming from the sky. There are a lot of rains in our city, and I used to enjoy observing the rain from my window.

I must say that I do not approve of water falling from the sky, not one bit! Water should remain in bowls, where it is meant to be, but clearly rain is a wicked form of water that has no respect for cats or our opinions.

Looking for shelter, I quickly discovered a small loft right under the roof I was sitting on. It was a narrow space, sheltered from all sides except one where the roof formed a tiny cornice. It was a dry and cozy place, with the soothing sound of rain on the roof, and I decided it would be a nice place to snatch a nap. When I woke up, it was time to eat, but I did not have any food.

I peered down from my lookout point for something that I could eat. The idea of getting into the garbage cans, like Mrs. Skunk did, was not appealing.

I noticed some little creatures below that resembled my old toys. I quickly went down and observed my prey. The back alley looked deserted, but I could not be fooled. I could smell all kinds of things but not see anything. Then, I spotted them!

A few birds were picking something from the ground. They looked like little chickens. For those of you who don't know, chickens are a type of food that hoomans will often share with cats, but these chickens were covered in feathers. I started slowly crawling towards them. All those days of practice at stalking "toys" paid off. With one jump, I got my meal. In the future, I would call this prey "silly birds," because they were so easy to catch.

I was only half-finished with my meal when an unusual creature approached me. It looked like a small barrel that had put on a mask and decided to go for a walk. It was Mr. Raccoon. He was extremely rude and began eating what was left of my food. It was not very nice, but having considered the size of his teeth, I decided I would let him have my leftovers and retreated to higher elevation. This was one of my first lessons that living outdoors is quite different from living in a cozy home with a Granny and Grandpa.

Over the next few days, I watched Mr. Raccoon closely. He slept all day in a tree at the end of our alley. By that time, I had been settled in my loft and marked the territory around it. Our back alley was part of Mr. Raccoon's hunting grounds, and to avoid further complications I had to give him a lesson.

One evening, Mr. Raccoon was passing by my shelter. He was terribly sure about himself, because nobody challenged him in our neighbourhood. He could not see me, but I was right above him, which is a good reason to always find a guard platform to perch on. I jumped on his back and sunk my claws in deep! Mr. Raccoon squealed and ran right down the alley.

Now I thought that he had learned his lesson, and I tried to dismount, but my nails were stuck in the thick fur on his back! Mr. Raccoon ran circles around the alley snorting and calling me all sorts of names I would not repeat in front of a polite audience. I bounced up and down on his back, yowling at him to slow down so I could get off, but he would not listen. I flapped in the wind in a most undignified manner as Mr. Raccoon ran around the alley.

All of the alley residents came out to see what the ruckus was about. Mrs. Skunk and her kids poked their heads out of the garbage can, the little skittering creatures poked their pointed faces from under the sewer grille, and even some silly birds flew down to sit on a wire and laugh at us.

Eventually, Mr. Raccoon got tired and slowed down, just enough for me to flop off his back, quite pooped from the ride. Quite pooped, but not too pooped to jump back up to my roof before settling down for a little grooming session. From that day forward, Mr. Raccoon would not walk over to my end of the alley, and I respected his tree and let him sleep in peace during the day.

Although I never found my way back to Melita's house, life in the alley was pretty good. We cats live in the moment, which is the best way to live, in my opinion. My quest for food kept me busy and I enjoyed many naps in my comfortable loft.

CHAPTER 6

Interactions with hooman neighbours

Our city block had several restaurants, all with back alley doors. Not too many hoomans visited the alley, but trucks and cars would come to the back doors. I missed my hooman companions, but became content with my street life.

After a while, hoomans who worked in the restaurants started noticing me. I was not invisible anymore! Some of them even put food and water for me near their doors. Hoomans are quite easy to train—all you have to do is to make them see you, and they can usually figure out how to get cat food and bowls of water by themselves with only a little bit of help. Meowing for a few hours twice a day is usually more than enough.

I love playing with hoomans. They are useful for providing cats with pats and food and taking care of our bathroom area. But I had mixed feelings about living with hoomans again.

My life on the street had changed me. I had become wiser and even protective of my place in the world. It is important to mark your territory when you live in an alley, and the best way to do that is to pee on a wall. I had been peeing in every corner of the alley, and it worked. Mr. Raccoon knew where not to go, and any other cats who thought the alley was unoccupied could check the corners and immediately know that this was the home of a very large and, I dare say, handsome cat.

But it was not a big surprise to me when the young man who worked in a place called "Greek restaurant" invited me to live in his home. Some hoomans have a good eye for cats, and once they see a top-notch guard cat, they tend to get attached and want to feed us and clean our litter boxes. It is only natural.

When I arrived in my new home, I made sure to mark my territory, peeing in all the corners of the house and other critical points. My new hooman did not seem to understand how important this was and kept getting upset, but as we all know, being upset with a cat is an unrewarding pastime.

He tried to offer me litter in a litter box, but it was different from what I was used to, and I did not care for it, not one bit. Besides, it was important to make sure none of Mr. Raccoon's cousins came into the house and ate our food.

After a short period of time, my new hooman seemed pretty upset and he took me to the cat shelter, which had an unusual name: SPCA. I think this stands for "Society for Petting Cat Always." It was an interesting place. I had never seen so many cats in one spot. We had plenty of food and water, and people who worked at this shelter were nice to us and did a good job of taking care of us.

Besides the staff, a lot of folks came to visit and play with us. Occasionally, some of the kitties were "adopted," which meant they left the shelter to live with a permanent hooman family. I liked to be at this SPCA and was not sure that I wanted to take my chances with another family who did not understand the importance of marking your territory. On the other hand, I was open to any opportunities that life might give me.

I noticed one family had been coming to our shelter regularly. Two grownups and a little girl walked around and looked at us. During one of their visits, my caretaker took me out of the cage and put me in the playroom, where I remained with this family. I really enjoyed playing with them. The little girl was good at throwing toys and they all had excellent cat-petting skills. In a few days, they came again and took me to their house.

I liked this new home and tried to make sure that it was truly mine; I began marking it all over. For some reason, my new family was not too happy with me peeing anywhere I deemed necessary. They tried to rearrange my toilet, took me for a walk in the backyard, and sighed a lot, but nothing changed. Then we started visiting different doctors. As I had known all along, nothing was wrong with me. Just life on the street had changed some of my behaviour forever.

But it took the animal doctors, who are called "veterinarians," a long time to figure it out. The veterinarians took samples of my pee and blood, which I graciously allowed them to do, to make sure I was healthy. Which, of course I was, being such a robust guard cat. They gave me some medicines to make cats less anxious, but I was not anxious. I am quite a confident cat, so they just made me sleepy, which is okay, because I am an expert sleeper.

I believe my adopted family really loved me, because the little girl was crying all the time. But I could not do anything to make everybody happy, and home security is important! One day, the little girl was crying while we visited yet another veterinarian. Her parents seemed sad as well.

Then the doctor, a big, smiling hooman who was expert at petting cats, came out to talk to the little girl and told her that I could live at the clinic. She was still sad, but she smiled and thanked the nice doctor, and that is how I came to be in charge of a veterinary clinic.

CHAPTER 7

Beginning of professional life

Pretty soon, I realized that the clinic was not only my new residence, but also my place of employment. All the staff treated me as an equal, and I immediately understood that my presence in the clinic was very important. My new home felt comfortable from the beginning, but I saw other animals in distress. I made sure to check in on every one of them. Just the sheer fact of my presence had a relaxing effect on the patients.

To me, the place looked magical. In the reception area were shelves loaded with food and treats that smelled awesome, and receptionists whose job was to pet me and lift me up or down to places when I meow.

I could not have imagined that I would have so many places to hide and so many cozy cushions to sleep on. It took me several days to explore the whole building. The hoomans in the clinic seemed clever and soon figured out how important I am. Our staff consists of doctors and nurses, technicians and receptionists, and also young people called "volunteers" who are there to learn what it is like to work in a veterinary clinic, and to brush my fur.

The doctors always look busy and either rush around or stand for long hours in the "surgery room," whatever that means. They do not have a lot of time to appreciate me, but they have their uses. They never have time to sit for long and often leave nice warm spots on chairs for me to nap on. They also use these things called "pens," which are a special type of cat toy that you can bite or smack out of their hand when they wiggle it over paper.

I like the nurses and technicians because they feed me every day, and they also do "laundry." This is when you take a bunch of towels and blankets from a dryer, and then build a warm pile of them for cats to sleep in.

The receptionist's duties we have already covered.

Shortly after my arrival, we had a staff meeting where I was the centre of attention. It was important to give me a proper name. To my delight, they quickly came to a conclusion that, given my noble nature and regal demeanor, as well as my long and well-known history of heroic exploits, my new name must be: Sir Lancelot. It was a big honour for them to be allowed to name me, and I worked hard to prove myself worthy of the new name.

We are busy during the day, but at night I am usually alone. There are many places for me to rest, but from day one I had my own bedroom in a large cat condo. I really like this location, but for some reasons my colleagues were locking the door to my cage. After everybody was gone home, it took me only few seconds to open the latch. Next morning our medical director was very upset about phone call he received at night: - "All door and windows are secure, but there is some movement inside". We have things called "motion detectors" in our clinic, and when security system is activated at the end of a shift any movement inside our office will create an alarm signal. It was nice that the security company learned that nice cat living in animal clinic is very smart too.

At the end of next shift they put a fastener on my door. Needless to say, that it took me only few seconds to untied it. I consider locking my cage as a game, and in the following days I was removing all kind of ties - rubber bands, nylon ropes just name a few. It was interesting when I found a metal bolt holding my room latch. There was a loud noise when this bolt hit the floor and I could wonder around again.

They have now custom made bracket to keep my door locked. It is working for the time being, but by the time you will be reading this, I will find the way to remove this device. I overheard a discussion about installing a padlock on my door, so now I observing the places when staff can hide the key and I'll be ready for any future challenge.

Occasionally, some other creatures stay in the clinic overnight, but they only stay in cat condos if they are cats. If they are dogs, they stay in dog condos, and if they are rabbits, then they stay in rabbit hutches. That way the hoomans can tell who is who. At least, I think that is how it works.

At the end of the shift, I always sit on top of a garbage container near the back door. My staff has to empty it every day before closing up the clinic. I like to remind them to leave me with fresh water and food.

My staff members sometimes bring their own pets to work. These are mostly dogs, which is a type of silly animal that pants a lot and smells funny. Many people will tell you that dogs are big and smell bad and have tails that smack into everything, and this is true. But if you can look past all that, there are many things to appreciate. For one, they are warm. They also typically respect cats, which is good. At least, most do, and the ones that don't are too slow to be much bother.

I have had an opportunity to spend many days in the company of dogs and have grown quite fond of them. Some are quite warm and comfortable to sit on. We never have any conflicts and treat each other with respect. I would say that some of them have even become my good friends.

CHAPTER 8

My mission

One of my first tasks was supervising the reception area. It was exciting to watch people entering through the front door with their pets. Dogs come mostly on a leash, but all other creatures arrive in some type of box called a carrier.

In my first weeks on the job, I was greatly surprised at the variety of different animals that visited our clinic. Cats and dogs were common, but I also saw rats, hamsters, ferrets, hedgehogs, turtles, snakes and more. Most of them I had never seen before and I was glad to expand my knowledge. Most cats were calmed by my presence, but some were so scared that they even hissed at me! As an official representative of the clinic, I just ignored such disruptive behavior.

My communication with the dogs was even simpler. They ignored me, and I did not pay much attention to them. All other creatures rarely needed my help; each and every one of them received full support from our medical personnel. Their hoomans often appeared in need of a cat to pet, though, so I kindly offered my head or flank, and that seemed to make the hoomans happy.

One aspect of my job I particularly liked. We had a jar with cat treats on the reception counter and my function was to test them before giving them to the patients.

Receptionists on duty are very busy. They must answer phone calls, talk to the owners and patients, push a lot of papers back and forth, work on something called a computer, and much more. It became clear to me that I should help my colleagues and protect them. too. To make their work easier, and less stressful, I let them scratch me behind the ears. I also have a cat bed on their desk and often nap there to improve office morale.

Some of our patients had strange habits. They would try to bite, scratch and do anything possible to harm our medical personnel. My mission was to educate the patients and enforce tabletop manners. It was not always easy, and I usually delegated this job to our nurses and technicians, but sometimes they needed rescuing.

There was the one time when I ran up the chief technician's back to save him from an angry cat, but in typical hooman fashion, he did not appreciate it. After that, I would be carried out of the room when the staff worked with aggressive cats. I do not mind delegating this work to them, since there is so much for me to do in other parts of the clinic, but sometimes I still try to sneak back to help them out.

Our treatment room has a lot of shelves and cabinets, so I liked to climb on top of them and watch what was going on. The only place I was not allowed to enter was Surgery Room, but not much was going on there anyway. Usually, doctors and nurses just standing around the operating table, looking at a sleeping animal. It is pretty boring, from my point of view.

But I like to help our patients after they are transferred to the recovery ward. I listen to their complaints and, I am sure, they feel better seeing me around.

It was also rather flattering to me to receive personal medical attention. When I first came to the clinic, I was measured, weighed, tested, and even looked at with something called "ultrasound." From then on, I would not worry about my health, because I was under constant care from my colleagues.

I have always had a hard time dealing with life when it becomes hot in the summer. I have a very thick and lustrous coat, you see, which I am quite proud of. It keeps me warm in the winter, and even keeps off the rain, which is important in my city. However, in the summer it gets so hot and muggy that all I want to do is sleep (even more so than is usual for a cat). During my first year at the veterinary clinic, my staff noticed this and that is when I had my first haircut. I was not too sure about it at first, since it is difficult to feel dignified when your beautiful coat is shaved, but it felt so nice! Many cats require sedation to have a proper haircut, as they find it quite stressful, but the head technician at my clinic has such a steady hand and reassuring manner that I allowed him to shave my lustrous hair, and since then we have had a very good working relationship.

Every time we receive new equipment, I see it as my duty to test it. This is true of ultrasound machines, dental machines and even x-ray devices. In addition to being a quality control officer, I also work hard every day on public relations. My teeth get cleaned every two or three years, so my breath always smells nice and my gums are as healthy as can be. This is important since I meet so

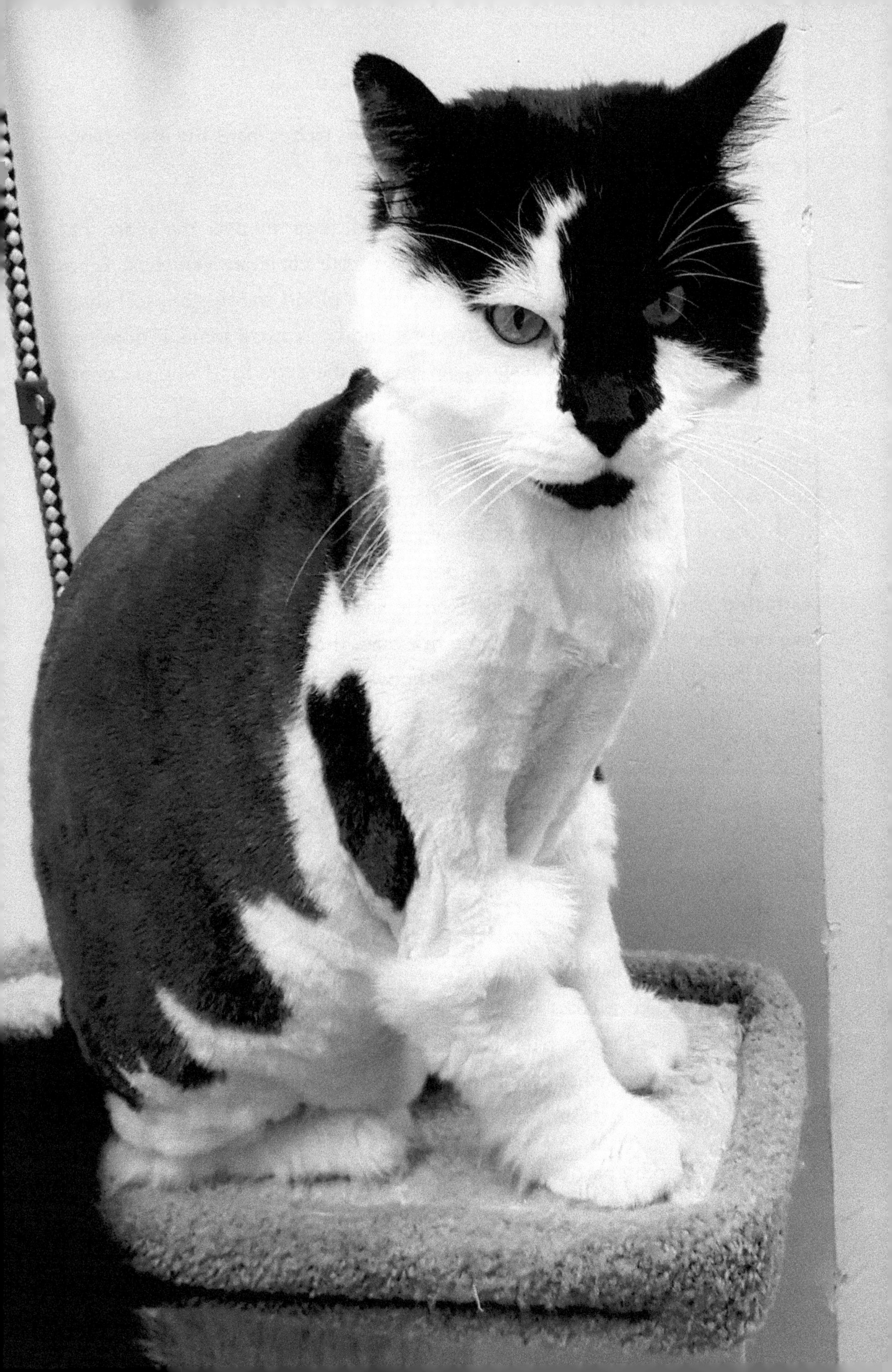

many hoomans and animals, and it demonstrates to hoomans the importance of proper dental care for their feline friends.

There is one more duty that I have performed diligently over the years that I am quite proud of. Some cats that come to our clinic are very sick. There is no chance of them getting better without a blood transfusion, so I share my blood with them. I am a big, strong cat and I can spare some. It does not bother me at all, and my colleagues always give me extra food when I donate blood, so everybody is a winner!

Recently, we had an interesting case. Somebody brought in a guinea pig with serious eye ulcers. No one could cure them and the poor thing was suffering. It is strange that this small creature is called "pig." It did not look like the pigs I knew. The big smiley hooman doctor took a little bit of my blood and extracted something called "serum" from it, and then he used this serum as an eye drop for the guinea pig. Within a few days, the guinea pig was cured. My blood literally saved this creature's life. I know now that I am a very important part of our clinic team, and it is no surprise that they call me "The Boss."

From time to time, we have pythons brought to us. They are basically a big, scaly noodle that sleeps all month and then wakes up hungry. They are the only animal that makes me nervous because my ancestors used to live in jungles where the pythons' ancestors would occasionally eat them.

My favourite of all the creatures that visited our clinic was a sugar glider, a small possum-like creature. I could not have imagined that such a funny animal exists. It looks like a cross between a squirrel and one of those skittering creatures who lived in the alley, but it can fly! I keep a close watch from the top of the cupboard whenever they are in the clinic because the nurses will not let me come any closer, despite my obvious interest.

I am so proud to be part of a team that helps animals and the hoomans who love them.

CHAPTER 9

Quality control

At first, I was overwhelmed by the quantity of cat food in our clinic. The week after I arrived, I spent a lot of time on the shelves where they stored the food. There were supplies for other animals as well, but I was obsessed with cat food.

Each bag had a different smell, and I began wondering if all these products were good for our patients. We could not expect hooman personnel to test the different foods; hence, it was clear that I was the best candidate for cat food testing. It was not an easy task. All bags were tidily sealed. It took me several days, or rather nights, to reach the contents of one bag. The food was delicious, and getting to it made me proud.

Next morning, I was surprised by my colleagues' reaction to my achievement. The chief hooman took me to his office and we had a long conversation, or rather, he talked and I listened. It was difficult for me to understand why he was so upset, and what he meant by "50 dollars a bag" and "nobody will buy damaged food bags." Pretty soon, we both understood that we had communication problems.

The hooman carried me back to the shelves of food, looked me in the eyes, and said, "Lance, no!" He repeated this phrase a few times, and I understood that I should not test the food from the shelves, and that my help was not appreciated. It was one of the very few conflicts I ever had with my employer. For the next two months, I continued eating food from the one bag I had so bravely opened. It was my luck that this food happened to be so tasty.

I have a great deal of respect for my employer, so I no longer test food bags... regularly. But on occasion, a bag just happens to get in my way and sometimes it looks a little bit suspicious, so I have to chew through one corner and try a little bit of the kibble inside. Just to make sure it is okay, you understand. I think the hoomans understand too, because even though they sigh and shake their heads in the morning, none of them appear at night when I do it, so it must not be that wrong.

Dr. Uri usually works in a small office at the back of our clinic when he is not with his patients. I like watching the doctor pushing the keys on a computer. The sound of it is mesmerizing. On one occasion, when the doctor's office was empty, I jumped on the table and tried to push the little buttons myself. It was not difficult, but my claws caught on some keys. I was enjoying pulling them out and wondered why my doctor could not extract the keys himself. They made such wonderful toys and are quite crunchy to chew on!

When Dr. Uri came back to the room, he tried to put the keys back, but it did not work. He did not say anything to me, just gave me "a look." He then picked me up and sat me on his lap and spent a long time petting me and looking at his well-chewed computer. From that day forward, the door to the doctor's office remains closed when he is not there.

I love my place, and to establish my presence, I had to mark it everywhere. My colleagues are so professional and understanding of my need to pee in different key locations. When I wanted to show appreciation to my favourite nurse, I even pooped in her shoes, so she would know how grateful I am. I like my doctors too, but never could find their footwear. Nobody attempted to punish me or even criticize, but for my part, I stayed consistent and kept marking the same places. The hoomans who work here are quite smart. They realize that you cannot change a cat, so now they just leave fresh towels every day in the spots I have designated, and I pee on those. Now, everybody is happy!

CHAPTER 10

I am not a "Puss in Boots"

Our clinic is always active in the community. We like to celebrate holidays and important local events. With my beautiful fur, I do not need any clothes, but once a year, when it is cold outside and the clinic is decorated with garlands and paper snowflakes, my colleagues put a red hat on my head that I wear for weeks. Sometimes it slides off and hangs down under my chin like a beard, but one of the receptionists usually notices and fixes this quickly.

I recently learned that the city I live in has a hockey team. I am not sure what hockey is, but hoomans talk about it a lot and get awfully excited. A few years ago, we had something called "the playoffs." This means everyone stands around all day and, instead of working, talks about "games" and "goals" and "penalties." But no one is certain of anything, and the conclusion is always that it is important to finish work on time so they can go home and watch... something. I find it all very confusing, but I wore a Vancouver Canucks scarf for the whole month anyway.

Speaking of clothes, during winter months we collect blankets, socks, gloves and scarves for people who are cold and don't have thick, lustrous fur like mine. The families of the pets who come to our clinic drop off all this interesting-smelling clothing and we put it into a box. Eventually, a nice hooman comes by to pick it up and take it to people who need it. While it is at our clinic, however, it is my responsibility. I like to guard this treasure trove by getting in the box and sleeping on top of the pile of clothing, adding a little bit of my hair to keep the people who will get it extra warm. I'm generous that way.

CHAPTER 11

I am in the movies

Recently, we started to make movies in our clinic. I had never seen any movies in my life, but I like the attention and the excitement of film production. It is easy to be a movie actor. One just has to be a cat. Some animal actors try to run away from the set, or do tricks, but most of them are dogs, and dogs are dumb. If they were just a cat, they would do fine. I do not mind being the centre of attention, and when you are in a movie, everyone is always looking at you, so that works out quite nicely.

Dr. Uri is also often in these movies, and sometimes other cats too. Sometimes Dr. Uri has to do tricks for the camera, since he is not a cat and has to work hard to be an actor. Luckily, he has me to help him with his tricks, so they always get done in one take, which is important when you have a veterinary clinic to run.

Another reason I like to get involved in video productions is the opportunity to spend time with my co-stars, Mr. Pirate and Clawdia. They are frequent visitors to the clinic, and we like to hang out together. Clawdia is a young cat who just wants to play all the time. She is very mischievous. Mr. Pirate, on the other hand, is a wise and well brought-up cat; he has travelled all over the world and been in many veterinary clinics. It is interesting to spend time with him and listen to his stories.

Our short videos are not just for fun. They teach hoomans how to understand other animals and how to take care of the cats, dogs and other critters in their life. This is important because not every cat can go see a doctor, and not every hooman spends years training to take care of cats (although they should).

Actually, my doctor said that only half of cats ever get to go see a veterinarian. I think this is really sad. So, we teach hoomans useful things, like how to tell if their pet is sick, and how to give them medication, and even how to choose the best name for their cat.

Dr. U. is always has his telephone with him and ready to help our staff with any issues. One day we all gathered in the reception area, when the doctor's telephone rang. It was call from one of our sister clinic and they had a complicated case, - constipated lizard. For those who don't know, lizards are curious things. I'd say they are like the little animals I used to hunt in the back alley, but they aren't warm, like they are supposed to be. They are room temperature, which is something I can sense with my luxurious long whiskers. They are also look like a sock, but one that moves around and hisses at you when you come near. Being a very educated cat, I eventually learned that they are a type of animals called a reptile and reptiles are 'cold blooded'. That is to say they cannot produce body heat and are always the same temperature as the world around them. Can you imagine that? I think it would be very strange to never be able to curl up into a warm ball and heat up a blanket fort, but apparently it works for them as there are a lot of reptiles out in the world, at least as many as there are proper animals like cats, which are called mammals. They also have scales instead of fur and whiskers, the poor things. But, despite all this strangeness we help them anyway because as the nice doctor says, all animals deserve our help, no matter how odd they are.

This poor lizard has not pooped in days, which as you can imagine is pretty uncomfortable. In the beginning I did not pay attention to this conversation, but then it became interesting. Most animal doctors do not learn much about reptiles in their schools. From what I heard they are spending many days studding cows and horses, but these big animals never come to our clinics. So in order to help a lizard, our nice doctor keep looking through giant and heavy books, and he looked to more books, and more books, until there was a huge pile of books on his desk and THEN he jumped up in excitement and yelled "I've solved it!". He realized that the lizard was living on sand, and ate a bunch of it by accident while eating his dinner, and how it might be stuck in his stomach. To find out what exactly is going on inside the lizard, doctor and his chief technician had to do something called X-rays.

When normal animals have x-rays done the technicians hug them to keep them calm so that the x-ray can be taken, but because lizards are too small to hug and too dumb to stay still when you ask them to, so the nice doctor and chief technician had to figure out how to do x-rays. What they did was they took sticky tape, and taped the lizard to a piece of cardboard, so he couldn't run away, and then x-rayed him and this is how it worked! Sure enough, there was the sand in the stomach, and doctor could see it on the x-ray. When veterinarians know what is wrong, they can proceed with treatment. We gave the lizard some mineral oil to drink, which he didn't like, but medicine often tastes bad but we still have to take it. The Oil helped the sand move, and then chief technician gave the lizard an enema, which is better, not talked about, but the lizard felt all better in the end.

Over the years I met a lot of various animals and as a representative of our clinic had good professional relationships with all of them. Some patients even became my friends, but only once I bonded with reptile. Her name was Masha and she was a tortoise. There are many different types of reptiles; snakes, pythons, lizards, turtles, and even crocodiles. It is a big family with some extinct relatives. I have mixed feelings about reptiles, and hope never to be close to some of them, but turtles are cool. They are a special type of reptile that carries a little house with them everywhere they go that they can hide in, which seems like a really sensible thing to do. I would not mind to carry my cardboard box with me if I could. For a long time I was confused different names hoomans are using for this reptile, turtle and tortoise. The way may see it, turtle lives mostly in the water and tortoise on the ground. Tortoises always seem so calm and are always walking around at a leisurely pace, but water turtles always look like they are swimming, which makes them very fast but not very graceful on land. By now you already understand that the tortoise is my favorite reptile.

Now let's talk more about Masha the tortoise. Her family brought her to us with cracked upper shell. We did not know how it happened. Maybe she fell or maybe someone stepped on her. We never learned. From the moment Masha entered the clinic she was very calm and confident. She started walking around with distinct knock of her shell against the floor- "ka-thump", because it wasn't straight. When offered food she immediately started chewing and was completely at ease. Everybody liked her. Our medical staff patched her shell with special compound called "rubber cement". It held the pieces of her shell together. It required several applications, so Masha stayed with us for many weeks. She had her own box, but was free to go any time. It was very easy to find her, because of the knocking sound she was often making.

Masha loved eat vegetables, especially cucumbers. She would run across the room, her shell making "ka-THUMP ka-THUMP ka-THUMP" noises as she did, to get a piece of cucumber whenever she saw one.

I liked watching her. She was brave and approached all animals and hoomans in our clinic without hesitation. Eventually her shell was healed but the edges never grew together quite the way they once were, despite the best efforts of the hoomans in our clinic, and so she always walked with a little thump every other step, but it didn't seem to bother her. Masha was picked up by her family once her shell was healed and they seemed really happy to have her back. I hope to see her again, when she comes to the clinic for a regular check up.

Our clinic is one of the few which taking care of reptiles. There is another type of reptile, called snakes, and the most common type of snakes we see are pythons. These are even stranger than lizards since they have no legs or paws or even ears! They look like a giant cat toy, but unlike cat toys they are not fun to play with since they are very strong and can get really, really big. I've never had any trouble from one, but something tells me that if we met in the jungle they might even be big enough to decide to turn a handsome and noble cat into a snack!

It takes a lot of special skills and knowledge to work with pythons safely. We even have "for pythons only" days. I like to watch them but only from a safe distance.

Pythons move with ease around the room despite the fact that they do not have legs. They can move forward in a straight line by stiffening their ribs, lifting a set of scales on their belly and moving them forward, so the loose ends grab the surface to push them ahead. I suspect they are much better swimmers than walkers.

Every python like to wind round their bodies around anything, and they like to hide. They are always wrapping themselves around the doctor's arms when he is trying to work with them and it is really funny seeing him and nurse trying to unwrap the python from around one of their arms, for the snake only to wrap around the other, and they have to keep going back and forth until they finally get it straight so they can do their jobs. There is always a lot of laughing as well as long, deep sighs whenever this happens.

Some pythons squeeze doctor's arm very hard. It can obstruct blood circulation and doctor has to squeeze his hand during examination in order to restore blood flow. From time to time pythons change their skin. We have several old skins in the clinic and I am not afraid to play with them.

Problem with pythons is that they always try to escape. Once they are gone, it is difficult to find them. Our staff is very familiar with python behaviors and usually finding the fugitive wrapped around a table leg.

Our doctors teach hoomans how to take care of snakes. They are very different from cats and all of their health problems come from either their food or their housing not being quite right. They are strong, animals, but I find it odd how easily they get sick if their house is too cold or too hot. I guess that is why it is nice to have a beautiful fur coat like me, so you don't have to worry about these things!

When one is watching the entrance door to our clinic, nobody can predict who will enter. Of course we have regular appointments, but occasionally something called "emergency" is happening. On this particular day very agitated lady with a towel in her hands ran in the door. I immediately felt a presence of a cat wrapped inside the towel. Within a few seconds doctor and technicians were in the reception area, and took a bundle with injured cat to the back room. Meantime cat owner told receptionist that Blackie is our regular patient and she was hit by a car. Should I mention that Blackie was a young girl-cat and was completely black except for a pair of huge, green eyes?

Our doctors are very good in saving animals life. They canceled all appointments for the rest of the day and were working on the Blackie in Operation Room. She came out of surgery with her leg in a cast. I had a chance to personally console Blackie only when she was transferred to the Intensive Care cage. Blackie's owner was very upset because she didn't' have money (whatever that is) to pay for her treatment and this is why she decided to abandon the cat and did not take her home. I do not understand why some hoomans can behave like that, but fortunately it does not happen very often. This poor kitty needed more surgeries and medical care to resume normal life. So Dr. Uri offered to take care of Blackie and find her a new home that could look after her once she was better. She lived in the clinic for a whole year, and had many surgeries, and all her injuries healed, except her leg. It was still sore after a year despite everything the nice doctor tried. The only solution to save Blackie's life was amputation of injured leg. This was a hard decision to make and the doctor spent a lot of time sitting with Blackie and petting her even though she didn't like him much and always hissed when he came near. At this time, the doctor had a cat. Luckily cats have four legs, so losing one isn't that big of a deal as we can still run and jump better than any hooman with just three!

She was very groggy and confused after the surgery. My presence helped Blackie to feel better. I explained to her that in order to preserve her life, the doctor had to remove her wounded leg. At the same time, I cheered her up with the story of my friend, a three-legged cat called Trinity, who lived with the Dr.U at that time, and who bossed around all the dogs and cats in the neighborhood and could jump up on top of the highest shelves in the house with ease. Blackie's recovery was going well and pretty soon she was stomping around the clinic on her three healthy legs. She became friendly with everyone, but she never seemed to care for the good doctor or appreciate what he had done for her. But that is ok, because all that matters in the end is that she got better.

That is how Blackie become my good companion. Our staff liked her too. As I mentioned she stayed with us for almost a year and fully adapted to use of her three legs. Blackie got special connection with one of our receptionists. When she decided to go back home, to Australia, Blackie joined her. He learned a lot about Australia from Mr. Pirate, one of our resident cats, he was born in the land of Down Under. We all liked to hear his stories of this exotic continent and strange animals that live there.

For me, the important thing is not that I am famous, but that our videos are helping living creatures and their hoomans all over the world.

Recently, there was talk in our clinic about "Andemic." My big smiley doctor made a movie about the importance of washing hands. I supervised the shot, because I have seen a lot of hand washing in my life. I was thinking about teaching cats proper grooming too, but then I remembered that all cats are perfect, which means they already know how to groom themselves perfectly.

There are a lot of things about the movie business I do not understand, but I was told that millions of hoomans have been watching me on YouTube, whatever that is. It pleases me that they can see me and feel happy about it. After all, I am a rather handsome cat and it would be a shame if they had to travel all the way to our clinic to see me. We get many letters from my fans, and I like listening to hoomans read them to me.

CHAPTER 12

My little friends

My friend Rookie is okay, even though he is a dog.

I have a number of special spots around the clinic where I like to spend my days. One of my favourite spots is on top of the reception counter. It has a view of a parking lot and at the same time I can keep an eye on the front desk. My colleagues have put a little cat bed there so I can be comfortable. Naturally, I stretch out on the counter and ignore it completely, but they know I appreciate the thought.

One day, when I was meditating on my counter and enjoying the view of Vancouver's grey sky, a little girl with her mother stopped in front of my window. They were engaged in a heated argument about me because they could not decide if I was a real cat or just a very well-made doll.

I always appreciate attention to my person and observed this situation for a long time. I also did not want to give them any clues and maintained my steely composure. Finally, the lady and her daughter gave up, and entered our clinic through the front door.

They politely asked our receptionist for permission before approaching me. Should I remind you that during this time I did not move at all, not even to blink my eyes. The little girl suddenly got very shy, but after gathering her courage, she carefully reached out her hand. Reached it out all the way up to the counter and... touched my whisker. Then she squealed and jumped away because she did not expect me to turn my head and say "purrr!"

Once the little girl got over her fright (the mother jumped a little as well), both visitors expressed their admiration for this cat's ability to stay so still. Little did they know this is a skill I developed long ago, hiding on my ledge above the alley and watching silly birds be silly. As has happened many times before (and after), the mother and daughter inquired about the possibility of taking me to their home to live with them. As usual, the receptionist explained that I am "The Boss" here and a valuable member of the staff. Despite their initial disappointment, we had a good time together. I even jumped on the girl's lap and gave her my best purr. The lady and her daughter left after a while and I resumed my duties.

The next morning, I was pleasantly surprised to see the same girl in front of my window. This time she was accompanied by her father. She was going to school and was excited to tell her classmates about me.

Her name was M... and she had already learned my name. This visit brightened my day.

It has been a long time since our first encounter, and M... comes to see me almost every day before going to school. She likes to share with me her news and dreams. I am a great listener and never interrupt my guests. I know all her plans and dreams, but I do not tell anybody. I also know that when she has school breaks or vacations, she cannot visit me, but she comes to see me once she is back at school. I am always here and happy to see my friend anytime.

When I think about my friendship with M..., it becomes clear to me that to maintain the cat and hooman bond, it is not necessary to live under the same roof. It is enough to think about each other, and then even if you do not see each other every day, you still keep a close connection in your heart.

Some cats stay with us regularly for a few days or weeks. This is called "boarding." If they are polite and well behaved, then they get to hang out with me around the clinic. This is Clyde, who has been staying with us for many years, and I always look forward to his visits. Clyde may look angry but he is not. He just looks cross all the time because his eyes are a little crossed. This is a picture of Clyde occupying my box, with my red towel, that my staff set out for me. Luckily, I am a gracious host, and that day there was a bonus box for me to occupy as well.

CHAPTER 13

I am a happy cat

Work in the veterinary clinic gives me a lot of time to think about life in general.

Some say I am one lucky cat, even if I do not believe in luck by itself (behind it always is a lot of work and determination).

Some would say I am the happiest cat in the world, and they would be right!

But the important thing is that I do not get luck and opportunity confused. As you can tell from this book, I am one hardworking cat. It is not easy to ensure the smooth running of the veterinary clinic, to connect hoomans and animals, and help our boarding cats feel at home, but I work every day to do my part to make it happen, and this makes me both happy and lucky. See how that works?

My life has given me many opportunities to learn important skills: From my Mom, I learned to be loyal; from Melita, the importance of caring for one another; from my life on the street, how to hunt and take care of myself; and from all the hoomans at the veterinary clinic, how to care for others.

I hope you have enjoyed reading the story of my life. I hope you now understand why I am a happy cat, and I know we have become good friends. So even if you live far away and cannot visit me at my clinic, I hope you will think of me sometimes, and that doing so will make you smile.

THE END

EPILOGUE

Every evening at 6 p.m. sharp, I sit on top of this garbage can to make sure that my staff remembers to feed me as they head out the back door to take out the trash.

ACKNOWLEDGMENTS

This project would not have been possible without the help of the dedicated staff of Arbutus West Animal Clinic in Vancouver, Beautiful British Columbia, Canada. Special thanks to Dr. Uri for his professional input and Chief Technician N.J. for his excellent photos and the great care he provides to our Hero. Also I have to acknowledge that Igor Burstyn (age 9) painted the portrait of Lancelot's "Mom".

ABOUT THE AUTHOR

Leo Burstyn is a semi-retired computer specialist living in Vancouver with his wife.

Leo was born and raised in a smaller agricultural town in the Southern Ukraine. From an early age he was surrounded by farm and domestic animals. When his two sons were growing up, they shared living space with dogs, cats, birds and even a tortoise.

You may call me Lance is his second book project. In 2018, Mr. Burstyn authored a book with Wilf Hurd about life in the Ukraine, entitled *Testaments from Kiev*.

Lightning Source UK Ltd.
Milton Keynes UK
UKHW030625301221
396391UK00007B/580

9 781999 104801